Your Native American NEIGHBORS

A Story Book for Coloring

Written by Gary Robinson
Illustrated by Jesse T. Hummingbird
© 2022 – Tribal Eye Productions

Special Thanks

I want to thank Jacque Nunez of **Journeys to the Past** for her valuable suggestions and revisions that helped improve the messages in this book. For more information about her Native American cultural education programs go to https://journeystothepast.com.

And a heartfelt thank you to Sandy Hummingbird for supporting this publishing project to keep Jesse's work alive for future generations. We will remember him always.

-Gary R.

Published 2022 – Tribal Eye Productions

P.O. Box 1123 / Santa Ynez, CA 93460

www.TribalEyeProductions.com

www.LandsOfOurAncestors.com

ISBN 978-1-7352003-5-4

Native Americans are the first people who lived in the land we call America. They have lived in groups called tribes or nations all over the country for thousands of years.

The different ways these Tribes lived their lives, the foods they ate, the homes they lived in, and the clothes they wore were all natural and fit perfectly with the places on earth where they lived. Those things are part of culture.

Many unique plants and animals exist in America that Native Americans know very well, so when settlers came here from Europe, Native Americans helped those colonists learn how to hunt for food and grow local vegetables. Sharing this knowledge was a kind gesture. Unfortunately, many of the first settlers treated Native Americans with hatred and disrespect.

As more and more settlers came, they began crowding out Native Americans and taking over places where they had always lived. These settlers believed European customs, languages, and religions were better than those of the Native Americans and formed a new country called the United States. Native Americans were mostly not included in the new country.

Many battles were fought because the settlers soon wanted all the lands where Native Americans lived. Many Native people died or lost their lives, lands, languages, and cultures.

Native Americans who survived the battles signed treaties with the United States to stop the fighting and were moved to areas called reservations. These were guarded places that were only a small part of the lands they once lived on.

In these treaties the United States promised to take care of Native Americans forever, but many Native people went Hungry or got sick. Life could be very hard on a reservation.

Even so, later, many Native Americans helped the United States
Win big wars against foreign enemies. In two World Wars, some
Native American soldiers used their tribal languages to
Send coded messages by radio so enemies wouldn't
Know what American soldiers were planning to do.

As time passed, Native Americans began learning how to do all kinds of jobs. Many had to move to cities to learn new skills to get these jobs. Others wanted to stay on their reservations close to where their families still lived.

But many Native Americans remembered their ancient ways of doing things. These traditions were passed on from generation to generation. The Elders taught their children and grandchildren those traditions so no one would forget them.

Finally, some tribes started businesses on their reservations to create jobs and provide income for their people. Some built factories. Others built restaurants. Still others built resorts, RV parks and campgrounds so tourists could visit Native American lands.

Many Native Americans studied to become doctors, lawyers, teachers, basketball players, artists and every other job you can think of. Now there are thousands of Native Americans doing these jobs all over America.

Nature and traditional activities are still important to many
Native Americans. Traditions are often remembered and
Carried on in private ceremonies but also with public
Events like powwows. Traditions include gathering
Plants for medicine, praying in a sweat lodge,
And speaking tribal language.

Today many Native Americans still live on reservations. But Many more live in small towns and big cities all across the country. Some may even shop in stores near you, be students in your class, or be your neighbors.

Now you know that Native Americans are still here, living
Their lives a lot like other Americans. Maybe it's
Time to meet your Native American neighbors!

One way to meet Native Americans is at a powwow, which is a social dance gathering usually open to the public. What Native Americans wear at powwows is called regalia, and they dance to honor their families, tribes, and traditions. They also celebrate who they are today and remember old ways of the past. If you go to a powwow, remember to always be respectful of others and their traditions.

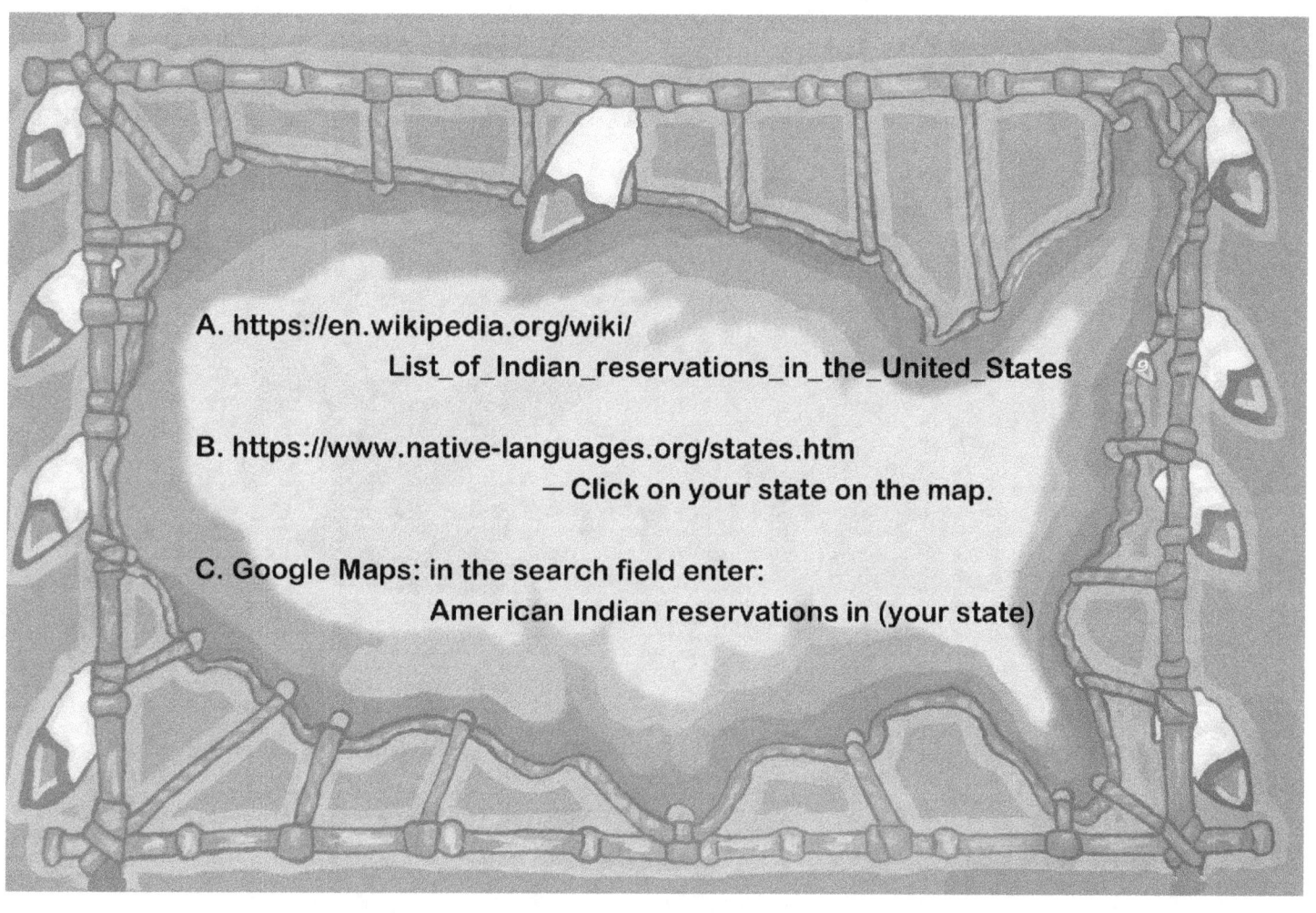

A. https://en.wikipedia.org/wiki/
   List_of_Indian_reservations_in_the_United_States

B. https://www.native-languages.org/states.htm
   — Click on your state on the map.

C. Google Maps: in the search field enter:
   American Indian reservations in (your state)

A parent or teacher may be able to help you discover
Native American communities near you by
going to one of the websites or locations
shown above.

Words to Know

Elders – Older people who have knowledge and wisdom about life because of their age, skills and experience.

Colonists – A group of people from another country who settle in a new country and take over the leadership of the people who already live there.

Culture – The beliefs, language, customs, and ways of doing things of a group of people.

Powwow – A Native American social gathering where men, women and children take part in traditional singing and dancing. The special clothing they wear expresses their tribe and family.

Regalia – Dance outfits worn by Native Americans at public powwows and for private ceremonies. These are not costumes.

Reservation – A section of land set aside by the U.S. government for a particular tribe or tribes. This land is usually only a small part of the large areas of land where tribes lived before Europeans came here.

Sweat lodge – A special ceremony for cleansing the body, mind and spirit and for praying for yourself and loved ones.

Traditions – Ways to do things that are passed down from one generation to the next. Traditions are part of a tribe's (or any group's) culture that may be thousands of years old.

Treaties – Agreements between two nations or governments that describe how the two will interact from that time forward. These are lasting agreements meant to be honored forever.

About the Author

Gary Robinson is a seasoned writer/author and filmmaker of Choctaw and Cherokee Indian descent. Much of his work has been about or on behalf of American Indian tribes, organizations, and businesses, creating documentary films, books, and educational materials about the histories, cultures, and contemporary issues of Indigenous peoples.

His other recent children's books include *Be Your Own Best Friend Forever*, *Native American Night Before Christmas*, and *Native American Twelve Days of Christmas*.

His teen novel *Standing Strong*, about a Suicidal Native teen girl whose life is transformed when she takes part in an oil pipeline protest to protect sacred Native American land and water, won the 2019 Moonbeam Children's Book Gold Award and was named one of the best books of the year by American Indians in Children's Literature.

About the Illustrator

Jesse Hummingbird (1952-2021) – Honored nationally by many in the world of art and recognized by his Cherokee tribe as a "cultural treasure" and "tribal elder," Jesse was born in Tahlequah, Oklahoma. He became a full-time artist in the 1980s, captivating the hearts of collectors and winning awards from multiple art museums, art markets and shows. "Artists and friends admired his work and respected him for staying true to his art and his Cherokee roots," Sandy Hummingbird said of her husband. "He will be missed by all who knew him."

www.ingramcontent.com/pod-product-compliance
Lightning Source LLC
Chambersburg PA
CBHW081159070526
44583CB00021B/2910